FAITH
IN A TIME OF PANDEMIC

BRUCE EPPERLY

Energion Publications
Gonzalez, Florida
2020

ISBN: 978-1-63199-462-3
eISBN: 978-1-63199-464-7

Energion Publications
PO Box 841
Gonzalez, FL 32560

https://energion.com
pubs@energion.com

TABLE OF CONTENTS

Introduction

The Living of These Days

This morning I arose before sunrise, went out on my patio and gazed at stars light-years beyond Cape Cod, Massachusetts, where I call home. A few hours later, after a time of morning meditation and writing, I headed to Craigville Beach for my daily walk. It was a glorious morning. Bright and cheery as the sun rose over Hyannis Port and Nantucket on the horizon. All was well with the world as I took my solitary walk. But this morning something was different. On my way home, I stopped at the local gas station to fill up a five-gallon gas can just in case the stations would be closed in the future.

This Sunday would be different. I would be broadcasting our worship service online. Our leadership had decided to suspend worship for the next two weeks, and then reevaluate our worship and programming activities due to concerns over COVID-19, the Coronavirus. I pondered as I began a two-week period, minimally, of self-sequestering with my family, apart from walks in the woods and beaches. Absenting from worship, meetings, eating out, and my favorite coffee house, I would be ordering my groceries online to be delivered at home later in the week. Life is different today. Even more so than the days following September 11, 2011. Our lives are physically and relationally smaller, and we are afraid.

We are coming to terms for what we hope is the temporary "new normal." We also fear that in some ways our lives will change forever. We know the dangers of denial. Governmental denial has rendered us unprepared for this crisis and our government is now playing catch up with medical tests, institutional regulations, vaccine research, and respirators. We have come to realize that fear is equally dangerous in not only suppressing our immune systems, poisoning our relationships, and destroying the fabric of society and government. As the day progressed and the governor of Massachusetts, the state where I live, called on the state to close restaurants, bars, and ban gatherings with over 25 persons, the reality of this "new normal" set in. In many households, denial and fear morphed

1

into depression and anger, and the reality that the world has radically changed and we weren't prepared for it politically, economically, spiritually, or emotionally. We are behind the curve and need to change our ways of thinking and action before it's too late!

1 John 4:18 asserts that "there is no fear in love, perfect love casts out all fear." As Thomas Paine says, "these are the times that try men's souls" — and not just men's souls! These are times in which faith and fear join in the quest for hopeful action and compassionate care in responding to real crises that threaten everything we hold dear. We can live by fear, closing the circle of love to include only those in our immediate families and letting the rest of the world go to hell. We can live also by love. Love that is prudent, but also generous and compassionate. Love that is careful, keeping proper social distancing, but also compassionate and sacrificial. Love that enlarges the soul and inspires us to patience and empathy, when we are tempted to be angry, impatient, uncivil, and uncaring, not just toward strangers but to those whom we hold most dear. As followers of Jesus and citizens in a time of pandemic, we are challenged as Abraham Lincoln challenged the USA during the Civil War, to follow the better angels of our nature, and to place our fears in God's hands, trusting God's presence in the direst situations and reaching out to the vulnerable, overcoming self-interest and leaning toward world loyalty. That isn't easy as we anticipate new regulations, personal and family isolation, and uncertainty about our economic system and social order. And, as we realize that there is nowhere to run or hide and that no community or nation stands alone anymore, immune from threat. We are all in this together.

Theology can cure or kill. In that spirit, let me begin with a negation that will pave the way to positive life-supporting theology: God did not cause the Coronavirus and is not punishing us for our nation's or our personal sin. Cause and effect are real: injustice, alienation, infidelity, and inhospitality have their costs to persons and communities. But this is not God's will. God wants us to have abundant life (John 10:10). God is present in our responses to the Coronavirus, inspiring us to greater love, guiding our footsteps toward service along with social distancing, and inviting us to care for one another. God is the fellow sufferer who understands our fear. God is also the loving companion who reminds us that love is eternal, and that we are held in God's care today, tomorrow, and forevermore.

Just one more thing. This morning as I was driving back from the beach, I observed the counsel highlighted on the marquee of our local fire department: "Facts, not fear." Accurate information has spiritual implications. The truth sets us free to act. Lies and distortions, especially when spoken by political leaders, fray the fabric of relationships and trust and can debilitate a nation. Facts are not always comfortable but they eventually liberate us from illusions, denial, and other counterproductive behavior. When we have the facts, we can make wise and reasonable decisions. We can be appropriately cautious and careful without panicking. We don't need politicians to spin facts to promote their agendas. Denial and underplaying risk lead to irresponsible and unwise behavior. Facts help us plan and alter our behaviors to support the wellbeing of ourselves and those around us. Facts alerted our church leadership to cancel worship services. It went against everyone's grain to cancel worship, but faithfulness, even when we have no symptoms, requires us to sacrifice our own plans for the greater good of the vulnerable around us and in our communities.

This book is a meditation on responding to the Coronavirus from a place of love, recognizing our fear and anxiety. Emerging as North Americans and Europeans were shaken for our illusion of safety and security, these words were inspired by my love for my congregation, South Congregational Church, United Church of Christ, Centerville, Massachusetts, my family on Cape Cod, my friends across the globe, and my own commitment to seek healing, most especially in difficult times. Let me assure you that it is alright to be afraid — I feel an undercurrent of anxiety as I write these words — but we don't need to be afraid of being afraid. Recognizing our fears, praying them, and placing them in God's hands will transform our lives, awaken us to our better angels, and enlarge our spirits in a time of pandemic, regardless of what the future brings. This is not wishful thinking or denial, but the affirmation that spiritual practices and healthy theological reflection enable us to gain a larger perspective on life — one that allows us to embrace the totality of our feelings, knowing that love is stronger than death and enabling us to discover that courage is fear that has said its prayers. In this time of pandemic, let us believe, with all our doubts, that nothing can separate us from the love of God! Let us discover that this is a time for kindness!

Let us begin our time with pausing to take a few deep breaths to center our spirits. In the Celtic tradition, there is a practice called the "caim" or "encircling." Standing, sitting, or lying down, either visualize or draw a circle around yourself, going in a clockwise direction, as you say a prayer for protection or guidance Just a few deep breaths expand our spirits from reptilian to global, from fear to kindness and hope. As you circle yourself, knowing that you are always in the circle of God's love, you may choose to repeat a scripture, say a prayer or recite a Celtic prayer, such as this portion of the Breastplate of St. Patrick:

> *Christ with me, Christ before me, Christ behind me,*
> *Christ in me, Christ beneath me, Christ above me,*
> *Christ on my right, Christ on my left,*
> *Christ when I lie down, Christ when I sit down.*

Continue to center yourself with this prayer: Let my living of these days be filled with hope and kindness. Let me feel my fears and place them in God's hands. Let this be a time for kindness and healing. Amen.

CHAPTER ONE

FAITH WITH ALL OUR FEARS

"I believe, help my unbelief." (Mark 9:24)

Author Madeleine L'Engle recalls a question she received following a lecture at a well-known Christian college. "Do you believe in God without any doubts," the student queried. To which L'Engle responded, "I believe in God with all my doubts." In reflecting on her journey of faith, L'Engle asserted that "those who believe they believe in God, but without passion in the heart, without anguish of mind, without uncertainty, without doubt, and even at times without despair, believe only in the idea of God, and not in God himself." In similar fashion theologian Paul Tillich claimed, that doubt is an essential part of faith. Tillich believed that if your experience of faith doesn't provoke moments of doubt, then you aren't taking your faith seriously.

I have come to believe that fear is also a necessary element of faith. If we trust the witness of the Psalms and the Hebraic prophets, anger, lament, protest, gratitude, and elation are also elements of faith.

We trust in God. We have experienced the power of prayer and the life-changing presence of grace. But our courage often vacillates when we are confronted by the internal and external storms of life. Like Peter, when we take our eyes off Jesus, the waves of fear overwhelm us and we sink into the raging sea (Matthew 14:28-33). The waves are real and we can drown. Denial of threat may lead to death. Caution is in order. But within the waves, there is a buoying force to lift us up and carry us to safety.

Intellectually, we know that God is our constant companion, the fellow sufferer who understands and the joyful ally who celebrates. We affirm that God is present in every moment of life as the source of comfort and challenge. At various times of our lives, God has made a way when we perceived no way forward. We can see the far horizons of grace, but we also must recognize the realities that threaten us. Yes, Peter was afraid and fear was a normal reaction, in fact a prudent reaction during a storm, but when he reached out to Jesus he found new strength and energy, enabling him to rise up and do what he believed impossible. I suspect he still was anxious, but as he took Jesus' hand, he could move forward faithfully despite the storm that surrounded him.

I must confess that I'm more than a little anxious these days as my newsfeed and the cable news cascade with reports of the advancing Coronavirus, the polarization that is tearing the fabric of national unity, and the increasing pace of global climate change. While I keep a calm exterior around my grandchildren and congregants, there is a maelstrom of anxiety within. I find that each day's news elicits feelings of anxiety as we have gone from "if" the Coronavirus will strike our neighborhood to "when" the virus will hit home. I have that middle of the night feeling: I'm sixty-seven and have medically treated hypertension. What if I get the virus? Will become incapacitated and need a respirator (or even be able to receive oxygen therapy due to a shortage of respirators)? Will my life be at risk? Will my grandchildren's life ever be the same after this?

Last week, with an abundance of caution, our congregation's leadership chose to suspend worship services and close the building for two Sundays, knowing that we may be closed for a much longer time. Yesterday, the local school cancelled classes for at least two weeks and likely longer. Now a child in our local school has shown signs of COVID-19 symptoms. Hundreds of thousands of USA parents and grandparents will become temporary home schoolers and other parents will have to choose between going to work and taking care of elementary school children. With a volatile stock market, the politicization of the Coronavirus, and the potential breakdown of medical infrastructure, will our nation's security and social order be at risk? Will I be able to provide pastoral care for my most vulnerable congregants? Will phone calls to the isolated and infirm be enough? Without regular Sunday services, will people discontinue contributing to our church, thus putting our church's ministry at risk?

The illusion of American exceptionalism and preparedness has been dashed into pieces as a result of the government's lack of preparedness for COVID-19 in terms of testing, treatment, and medical supplies. It is evident that neither an ocean nor a border wall can protect us from contagion. Nor can nation-first policies ensure national security in an interdependent world. We feel at the mercy of powers beyond our control. Our uncertainty about the future manifests itself in ambient anxiety, impatience, and anger. Social distancing is making hermits of us all, and many of us are forced to be with our "loved ones" far longer than is comfortable. Yet, in the storm of pandemic, there are also signs of community and compassion, albeit in new and creative ways. Like you, I am reaching out to friends and congregants by phone, email, texts, and platforms for visual contacts.

The Gospel of Mark describes the story of a storm at sea. It was a beautiful day when Jesus and his followers set off across the Sea of Galilee, but then out of nowhere, the sky darkened, lightning struck and thunder crashed. As Mark notes:

> A great windstorm arose, and the waves beat into the boat, so that the boat was already being swamped. But Jesus was in the stern, asleep on the cushion; and they woke him up and said to him, "Teacher, do you not care that we are perishing?" He woke up and rebuked the wind, and said to the sea, "Peace! Be still!" Then the wind ceased, and there was a dead calm. He said to them, "Why are you afraid? Have you still no faith?" And they were filled with great awe and said to one another, "Who then is this, that even the wind and the sea obey him?" (Mark 5:37-41, AP)

After all, they had experienced as Jesus' partners in ministry, in a moment of crisis, Jesus' followers felt powerless and at the mercy of natural elements beyond themselves. In their fear, they forget that the miracle worker, their savior, was with them and that with Jesus as their companion, no storm could overwhelm them.

Without getting into the metaphysics of the miraculous, I see three "miracles," or extraordinary acts of divine power in this story. First, God's presence was revealed in the experiences of the disciples. The storm continued to rage, but once they realized Jesus was with them their fear was placed in the larger perspective of God's compassionate presence. The storm did not immediately cease, yet their own fear subsided. Second, within the raging storm, they

7

discovered a place of calm. Jesus was in the boat, hidden in their spirits. When Jesus says "peace, be still," he is speaking both to the disciples' emotional maelstrom and the raging storm. The loving energy that brought forth the big bang could also move within the wind, rain, and their own fear and trembling. Third, in ways we cannot imagine, Jesus' spiritual calm and centered spiritual energy restored calm to the physical environment, enabling the disciples to safely reach the shore.

Reading the Bible isn't for the faint-hearted or those who want to escape the challenges of life. Much of scripture emerged in times of political and personal conflict. Even in the best of times, national unity is at risk and temptation lurked behind every corner. Listen to these words from Psalm 46. They sound as familiar as this morning's headlines or a presidential news conference.

God is our refuge and strength, a very present help in trouble.
Therefore we will not fear, though the earth should change,
    though the mountains shake in the heart of the sea;
    though its waters roar and foam,
    though the mountains tremble with its tumult.
There is a river whose streams make glad the city of God,
    the holy habitation of the Most High.
God is in the midst of the city; it shall not be moved;
God will help it when the morning dawns.
The nations are in an uproar, the kingdoms totter;
    he utters his voice, the earth melts.
The Lord of hosts is with us; the God of Jacob is our refuge.
Come, behold the works of the Lord;
    see what desolations he has brought on the earth.
He makes wars cease to the end of the earth;
    he breaks the bow, and shatters the spear;
    he burns the shields with fire.
"Be still, and know that I am God!
    I am exalted among the nations,
    I am exalted in the earth."
The Lord of hosts is with us; the God of Jacob is our refuge.

The Psalmist vacillates between anxiety and trust. The old order is collapsing. The future is uncertain. Will Jerusalem survive the onslaught? Yet, the Psalmist finds perspective. The God of Jacob, the One who saves the helpless, is with us. Then, in the quiet center of the political and social cyclone, the Psalmist finds peace. "Be still and know that I am God." There is stillness in the storm. There is a place where fear finds love and anxiety is transformed into action. That place is the still point where God's Spirit and our spirits meet, where we discover in the most difficult situations that God is a lively healing circle whose center is everywhere and whose circumference is nowhere.

Don't Be Afraid of Being Afraid. A young child regularly experienced night terrors, a sleep disorder causing feelings of dread and panic. He was fearful of going to sleep alone. At their wit's end, their parents made an appointment with a psychiatrist, who spent an hour drawing pictures, playing games, and talking with the child. At the end of the session, the psychiatrist sat down with the child and his parents and told them that nothing was wrong but that "the most important thing is for them to not be afraid of being afraid."

Fear, like grief and anger, are emotions and there are good reasons to feel these emotions. The Hebraic prophets were righteously angry at the realities of injustice, poverty, and idolatry in the Northern and Southern kingdoms of Israel. Jesus was filled with righteous anger as he over- turned the tables in the Temple marketplace, protesting religious practices that gouge the poor and fill the coffers of religious leaders. Those of us who lose parents, siblings, children, spouses, and dear friends, can feel tremendous grief. Healthy grieving involves embracing your pain and anger and not denying the loss you are experiencing. In the same way, fear is an authentic response to a threat — whether it be the uncertainty of the Coronavirus, predictions related to global climate change, or the sound of footsteps trailing you on a dark street. When the angels tell Mary and Joseph, "don't be afraid," they are not counseling them to deny their feelings but inviting them to trust God despite their fears. Denial is just as debilitating as hopelessness. When we embrace our fears, we feel the depth of our emotional lives. In embracing our whole selves, light and darkness, heroism and cowardice, courage and fear, we awaken to God's healing and empowering presence. Mary, Joseph, and the shepherds were afraid, but out of the fear came agency. Mary opened her whole self to a miraculous birth. Joseph chose to affirm Mary's pregnancy. No longer afraid, the shepherds raced to give homage to the Messiah. American poet Karle Wilson Baker affirmed that "courage is fear that has said its prayers." Today, I recognize that I am afraid, as I hear of the first case of COVID-19 on Cape Cod, where I live.[1] I am concerned as an active pastor and grandparent when I hear from infectious disease specialists that closing the schools and churches for two weeks is insufficient and that we will be in lockdown for more than a month to fully respond to the virus. I worry about the future of my aging congregation, how I will conduct pastoral ministry, and my ability to homeschool for the indefinite future not to mention the impact of the pandemic on my grandchildren's lives. Yet, when I say my prayers, I feel a connection with a Deeper Love and Power than my own. I no longer feel alone. I feel connected with God, with those for whom I pray, and for the planet and its peoples.

Be afraid, knowing that fear like doubt, is not an impediment to faith but an affirmation of the wondrous fragility of our lives and the lives of those we love. Fear can lead to life-saving action. Let your fear open your heart and mind to compassion and creativity, and appreciation of your one unique and precious life.

Practicing Our Faith in a Time of Pandemic

African American theologian and spiritual guide Howard Thurman (1899-1981) describes a childhood experience of divine guidance in the middle of a thunderstorm. It was hot August day and Thurman went berry picking in the woods behind his family's home in Daytona Beach, Florida, stuffing as many berries in his mouth as his pail. His orgy of berry picking was interrupted by a flash of lightning and crash of thunder. As darkness, punctuated by lightning strikes, descended, Thurman realized he had no idea where he was. Panic-stricken, his first impulse was simply to run — in any direction! Then he remembered something his grandmother told him, "When you don't know where you are, stop, look, and

---

1   March 13, 2020.

listen." So, Thurman stood still. With the first lightning strike he looked to the left, with the second he turned to the right, with the third he looked behind, and finally he looked ahead until he something familiar emerged. As he walked toward the familiar spot, he paused to wait for the next lightning strike, until he found his way home. Within the storm was the pathway home. In pausing and noticing, Thurman found his bearing, transforming fear into focus and panic into prayer.

The Psalmist says, "be still and know that I am God." In this exercise, begin with a time of silence, calming and centering your spirit. In the quiet, no longer ruled by the reptile brain, the fight, flight, or freeze response, reflect on your fears related to the Coronavirus. Identify your deepest concerns for yourself, your loved ones, and your community. Don't deny your fears, simply notice.

In the next step, once again, pause quietly and notice a Deeper Wisdom flowing through you with each new breath. Awaken to divine guidance as you ask God how best to respond to your fears. What first steps can you take to move from fear to agency and panic to calm? See yourself as an actor, liberated from the bondage of fear, and empowered to celebrate your unique and gifted life and serve God in our relationship with others. Let recognizing your fear expand your empathy for others and your willingness to safely and appropriately support them in this time of pandemic.

Loving God, there is so much of which to be afraid. I bring my fear, uncertainty, panic, and anxiety to you. I place my whole self, fear and courage alike, in your hands. Use my fears and anxiety as instruments of grace and empathy. Transform my fear to action that I might serve you in this challenging time, giving glory to you and beauty to the world. Amen.

CHAPTER TWO

FAITH THAT HAS SAID ITS PRAYERS

Rejoice in the Lord always; again I will say, Rejoice. Let your gentleness be known to everyone. The Lord is near. Do not worry about anything, but in everything by prayer and supplication with thanksgiving let your requests be made known to God. And the peace of God, which surpasses all understanding, will guard your hearts and your minds in Christ Jesus. Finally, beloved, whatever is true, whatever is honorable, whatever is just, whatever is pure, whatever is pleasing, whatever is commendable, if there is any excellence and if there is anything worthy of praise, think about these things. Keep on doing the things that you have learned and received and heard and seen in me, and the God of peace will be with. I know what it is to have little, and I know what it is to have plenty. In any and all circumstances I have learned the secret of being well-fed and of going hungry, of having plenty and of being in need. I can do all things through him who strengthens me. (Philippians 4:4-9, 12-13)

In times of transition and crisis, having a regular schedule is essential to physical, emotional, mental, and spiritual health. For some who will be homebound, this means telecommuting not just on an ad hoc basis, but with regular hours including a lunch break. It may mean dressing for work rather than working from home in your pajamas and bathrobe. Since the local Cape Cod schools have been closed for two weeks, minimally, beginning March 16, 2020, it means that I will continue my usual practice of rising at 4:30 a.m. for prayer and meditation, write or study for an hour or so, go to the beach before I pick up the first boy around 9:30 a.m. to read and do math. His parents will do a boy exchange after lunch and I will do the same with the second boy until 4:00 p.m., when I will have my Zoom online evening prayer service for church members. I will continue my sunrise beach walks, pastoral care, writing, and preparation for lectures and sermons that may be cancelled or preached via social media. Boys 9 and 7, like all children their age, need regularity to minimize anxiety. The same obviously applies to teens, college students, and adults.

In a similar fashion, we need regularity in our spiritual lives. In Philippians 4:4-9, Paul gives one pattern for our spiritual lives. While there are one hundred ways to kneel and kiss the ground, as the Sufi mystic Rumi avers, finding the path that fits our schedule and spiritual lives is essential. Spiritual practices need to flow with our lives rather than go against the current of our personality, time schedule, family life, and professional responsibilities. Paul's counsel is powerful since his words come from a jail cell and not a comfortable home.

From Paul's perspective, spiritual practices are ultimately grounded in joy and thanksgiving. While we cannot conjure up joy, we can practice joyfulness even if we aren't yet joyful. We do this by looking for God's presence in both pleasant and challenging situations, speaking words of affirmation and comfort, and noticing beauty rather than ugliness. Thanksgiving is essential to all-season spiritual growth. Thanksgiving is grounded in the faithful and loving interdependence of life. Counting our blessings reminds us of the goodness of life despite our challenges. Thanksgiving opens us to the future, enables us to face adversity, and encourages persistence. In our gratitude, we can recite along with the late UN General Secretary Dag Hammarskjold:

For all that has been — *thanks!*
For all that shall be — *yes!*

Thanksgiving gives birth to the "yes" of hope — the fierce urgency of hope — in a time of pandemic. The God who has been our "help in ages past" will be "our hope in years to come." Connected with God, we can feel free to ask, seek, and knock, to petition for our own needs and intercede on the behalf of others. The regularity of spiritual patterns such as these provide ballast in a time of uncertainty and helps us face unwelcome change trusting God and our own resilience. In trusting the gracefulness of God moving through our daily lives, we are inspired to join an abundance of caution with a greater abundance of love!

Paul challenges us to live affirmatively. "Finally, beloved, whatever is true, whatever is honorable, whatever is just, whatever is pure, whatever is pleasing, whatever is commendable, if there is any excellence and if there is anything worthy of praise, think about these things."Not denying the threat — and Paul often experienced conflict and threat! — we also do not need to succumb panic or despair. For those of us who regularly tune in to the "breaking news," it's easy to assume that we are powerless in the face of the looming threat. The Coronavirus becomes the only reality. As the Breton prayer says, the sea is so large and my boat is so small! Affirmations paint a larger picture of reality in which in partnership with God we have the resources to face pandemic, personal reversals, and our own mortality. Paul's Letter to the Philippians is a treasure chest of spiritual affirmations, which can be invoked in every season of life:

> *The good work God has begun in me will be brought to completion by Jesus Christ.* (1:5)
> *I have the mind of Christ.* (2:5)
> *God is at work in my life so that I will serve God and the world.* (2:13)
> *I shine like a star through God's grace.* (2:15)
> *With eyes on the prize, I press toward the goal of salvation* (3:14)
> *I can do all things through Christ who strengthens me.* (4:13)
> *God will supply all my needs.* (4:19)

This is the power of affirmative faith, enabling us to face the pandemic with courage and wisdom, recognizing that we have the power to shape our lives regardless of the circumstances.

Practicing Our Faith in a Time of Pandemic

Everyday practices can transform our lives, moving us from fear to love, and placing our fears in the context of God's mercy. During this time of pandemic, let us, in the spirit of Therese of Lisieux and Mother (Saint Teresa) of Calcutta, do ordinary things with great love.

Washing Your Hands. The Zen Buddhists say that "before I was enlightened, I chopped wood and carried water. After enlight-

14

enment, I chopped wood and carried water." Ordinary actions can be portals into holiness. Thin places where heaven and earth meet are everywhere for those awake to the ever-present, ever-active, ever-loving God. During this time of pandemic, we are counseled to wash our hands regularly for twenty seconds. We have been counseled to sing "Happy birthday to you!" twice. We can also use this time as a spiritual ritual. For example, you can sing the Doxology:

Praise God, from whom all blessings flow;
Praise Him, all creatures here below;
Praise Him above, ye heavenly host;
Praise Father, Son, and Holy Ghost. Amen.

You may choose a more inclusive version as you wash your hands, such as a version from the United Church of Christ:

Praise God from whom all blessings flow;
Praise God, all creatures here below;
Praise God for all that love has done;
Creator, Christ, and Spirit, One.

After a few deep breaths, you might wash your hands, saying the Lord's or Our Savior's Prayer or a version of the Jesus Prayer:

Lord, have mercy upon me.
Christ, have mercy upon me.
Lord, have mercy upon me.
(with deep breaths between each phrase)

Another option is a short breath prayer from one of my spiritual mentors, Congregational pastor Allan Armstrong Hunter:

I breathe the Spirit deeply in
And blow it peacefully out again.
(repeat three times slowly)

Many persons have found strength in reciting the Lord's Prayer or Psalm 23, both of which take about twenty seconds to say.

Remember that this pandemic is a time for kindness, so reach out safely and with appropriate social distancing to persons in need and persons in your community of faith. Greet the letter carrier and other service persons with smiles and patience, blessing them in your heart or words.

Living by Affirmations. Throughout the week, repeat the affirmations from Philippians. You may choose to write them down, reading throughout the day. You may also simply repeat which one comes to mind. In reciting affirmations, you begin the process of healing your mind and releasing yourself from self-imposed limitations. Try to repeat each affirmation ten times each day and whenever you begin to feel angry, impatient, and fearful in the face of the pandemic. Here again are Paul's spiritual affirmations, cited above:

> *The good work God has begun in me will be brought to completion by Jesus Christ.* (1:5)
> *I have the mind of Christ.* (2:5)
> *God is at work in my life so that I will serve God and the world.* (2:13)
> *I shine like a star through God's grace.* (2:15)
> *With eyes on the prize, I press toward the goal of salvation* (3:14)
> *I can do all things through Christ who strengthens me.* (4:13)
> *God will supply all my needs.* (4:19)

Sabbath Time. Restrictions on travel and social interactions can be inconvenient. They can also be a grace note in a busy life. Many Facebook friends have pondered the closings of schools, churches, workplaces, libraries, and public places as an invitation to Sabbath. Telecommuting can also change our experience of time. While parents and grandparents whose children and grandchildren are at home may have trouble finding Sabbath, even in their lives there can be a slowing down, especially as parents and grandparents, aunts and uncles, are able to take turns in childcare.

In this Sabbath time, take to slow down. As spiritual guide Gerald May counsels: pause, notice, open, yield to the experience of the moment, and respond to God's call. Let the busyness of carpools to work and sporting events subside and experience the Everlasting Now of this Holy Moment. Sigh deeply, letting go of tasks that can't be done and opening to a deeper state of rest. Rest in God's presence, trusting past, present, and future to God's care.

16

Holy One, Parent of Jesus and All Creation, grant us your peace. Let every breath be a prayer. Let me do ordinary things with love. Let this be a time for kindness. Amen.

CHAPTER THREE

ALL THE WRONG ANSWERS

As Jesus walked along, he saw a man blind from birth. His disciples asked him, "Rabbi, who sinned, this man or his parents that he was born blind." (John 9:1)

Theologians and pastors alike must take seriously the Hippocratic counsel, "First, do no harm." During times of crisis, unhealthy theologies proliferate, harming most especially the most vulnerable among us. Hurricane Katrina was blamed on New Orleans LGBTQ+ community, despite the fact that the "immoral" French Quarter fared much better than many of the conservative Christian churches in the city. HIV/AIDS was touted as God's punishment of decadent America, even though children and young people like Ryan White and my Georgetown University student Paul were among its victims. Job's friends who previously described him as the most moral of humans condemned him as dishonest and evil, counseling him to repent his sins to receive personal and economic restitution.

The emergence of the Coronavirus is no exception to the proliferation of heartless theologies, which blame victims, rather than seek solutions. Megachurch pastor and advisor to President Donald Trump Robert Jeffress asks, "Is the Coronavirus a Judgment from God?" waffles in his response, but ultimately attributes the virus to consequences of Adam and Eve's original sin.[2]

Another megachurch pastor Pastor Rick Wiles, Flowing Streams Church, Vero Beach, Florida, claimed that the coronavirus is God's "death angel," blaming parents "transgendering little children" and "the filth on our TVs and our movies" for what he views as divine judgment and calling Americans to "get right with God."[3] Perhaps it is the pastor and all those who believe in transactional, acts-consequences forms of divine punishment who need to "get

---

2 https://www.firstdallas.org/blog/is-the-coronavirus-a-judgment-from-god.
3 https://www.newsweek.com/christian-pastor-claims-coronavirus-gods-death-angel-blames-parents-transgendering-little-1484473.

right with God" and quit taking God's name in vain by identifying catastrophic events like HIV/AIDS, Hurricane Katrina, cancer, and COVID-19 with God's will or the direct action of an angry God!

Biblical Understandings of Divine Punishment. Robert Jeffress' question, "Is the Coronavirus God's Judgment on America" points us to one of the most significant theological questions, popularized by two other questions, "Why do bad things happen to good people?" and "Why do good things happen to bad people?" All of us, including the authors of scripture, seek an explanation for the apparent "slings and arrows" of fate. We want the universe to make sense. We want to find a cause or someone to blame for our misfortunes. A totally random universe leaves us uncertain morally and spiritually. Many of us want good to pay off and evil to be punished. That calculus is at the heart of the acts-consequences vision of Deuteronomy 28. Those who follow God's way will be blessed economically and politically:

> *Blessed shall be your basket and your kneading bowl.*
> *Blessed shall you be when you come in, and blessed shall you be when you go out all these blessings shall come upon you and overtake you, if you obey the LORD YOUR GOD:*
> *Blessed shall you be in the city, and blessed shall you be in the field.*
> *Blessed shall be the fruit of your womb, the fruit of your ground, and the fruit of your livestock, both the increase of your cattle and the issue of your flock.* (Deuteronomy 28: 2-6)

In contrast, those who turn from God's way will be cursed in all the affairs of their lives, suffering God's righteous judgment:

> *The Lord will send upon you disaster, panic, and frustration in everything you attempt to do, until you are destroyed and perish quickly, on account of the evil of your deeds, because you have forsaken me. The Lord will make the pestilence cling to you until it has consumed you off the land that you are entering to possess. The Lord will afflict you with consumption, fever, inflammation, with fiery heat and drought, and with blight and mildew; they shall pursue you until you perish.* (Deuteronomy 28:20-22)

19

In the orderly universe, portrayed by the authors of Deuter-onomy, good and evil are punished equitably. Every person and nation get what they deserve, whether in terms of military victory, good health, accidental death, cancer, poverty, wealth, or a child's terminal illness. God's judgment falls upon evildoers and God's blessings fall on those who follow God's way. Wealth, success, and health are signs of righteousness. Poverty, failure, and disease signify immorality.

The Bible is a library of texts, reflecting many theological positions as well as an evolution in our understanding of God's presence in the world. While the book of Job doesn't provide a comprehensive explanation of the "problem of evil," Job challenges the linear acts-consequences understanding of rewards and punish-ments found in popular religion and grounded in the counsels of Deuteronomy 28. The most righteous of persons loses everything — children, wealth, social status, and moral standing. Job protests his innocence, challenges superficial understandings of suffering, and even files a spiritual lawsuit against God.[4]

Jesus further challenges the linear understanding of wealth and poverty and health and sickness in the Sermon on the Mount and suggests, much to the chagrin of those who claim to be morally superior, that God's love embraces righteous and unrighteous alike.

> You have heard that it was said, "You shall love your neigh-bor and hate your enemy."
> But I say to you, Love your enemies and pray for those who persecute you, so that you may be children of your Father in heav-en; for he makes his sun rise on the evil and on the good, and sends rain on the righteous and on the unrighteous. For if you love those who love you, what reward do you have? Do not even the tax collectors do the same? And if you greet only your brothers and sisters, what more are you doing than others? Do not even the Gentiles do the same? Be perfect, therefore, as your heavenly Father is perfect. (Matthew 5:43-48)

God's perfection is found in God's loving embrace for all hu-mankind, "good" and "evil" alike. Good and bad fortune occur

---

4 Bruce Epperly, *Finding God in Suffering: A Journey with Job* (Gonzales, FL: Energion Publications, 2014).

apart from our personal morality. They are not the result of God's specific judgment on persons based on their morality or place in society. God's blessing and care apply to all. Jesus does not deny that our actions have consequences. In Matthew 25, God's judgment of nations relates to how political and economic policies respond to the "least of these." Cause and effect exist both in our personal and political lives. The United States is still bearing the burden of nearly four hundred years of genocide, slavery, and Jim Crow policies. In our personal lives, smoking and obesity are risk factors for cancer and heart disease, and dysfunctional parenting harms children, giving birth to their own dysfunctional parenting, apart from loving and therapeutic interventions. This is not, however, the result of a linear, one-to-one understanding of divine punishment or God's will. God is out to love us, not to hurt us. As Paul says in Romans 5:8, "God proves his love for us in that while we were still sinners, Christ died for us." Grace welcomes righteous and unrighteous alike, welcoming us home and providing the healing we need! In fact, as the apostle Paul asserts, "no one is righteous; not even one" (Romans 3:10). We all need grace, and our good or evil behaviors, like our health and illness, are the result of many factors and not just our attitudes or behaviors. We are joined in a fabric of relatedness in which no one is set apart, and everyone depends on God's grace and the goodness of others for their wellbeing.

When Jesus was asked "why was this man born blind?" he, like the author of the Book of Job, challenged the acts-consequences vision of health and illness, and wealth and poverty. Neither than man nor his parents sinned! Instead, Jesus proclaimed that the healing will be a catalyst to inspire people to give God glory, placing God at the center of their lives and living their lives according to God's vision and not their own self-interest. Then, Jesus reminded his followers that we must work while it is still daytime. The solution to the problem of evil is not abstract. It is found in companionship with God and doing God's work concretely responding to the suffering of those around us. Pain is a call to compassion. Loneliness an invitation to relationship. Injustice a call to protest. As June Jordan says, in her "Poem to the South African Women," "we are the ones we have been waiting for" in what Martin Luther King described as "the fierce urgency of now." In this crisis moment, God urgently needs us to be images of hope and agents of compassion bringing God's realm to birth on earth as it is in heaven.

What Kind of God? We have heard the wrong answers. Coronavirus and AIDS are God's punishment for our sins. Another wrong answer is that health and illness are entirely a result of our previous actions. I believe -and have discussed this in other books - that other wrong answers include:

- God predestines every event, positive and negative, salvation and damnation.
- God causes every event, eliminating human agency, thus making God the real-time cause of cancer, HIV/AIDS, Coronavirus, earthquake, and tidal wave.
- God is completely unrelated to the world, the "unmoved mover," immune to both joy and suffering, apathetic and beyond the world of change.
- God creates the world, like a watch maker, and leaves it entirely to its own devices.
- The future is already decided and we have no role or agency in shaping history.

I believe that God is, in contrast, the "most moved mover," dynamically and providentially present in our lives, guiding us and the events of our lives and encouraging us to use our real freedom and creativity to be God's companions in healing the world.[5] God is the fellow sufferer who understands, who empathetically experiences our fear and anxiety, and pain and suffering, from the inside. Involved in the affairs of our lives, God feels our uncertainty about the progress of the Coronavirus and fear that it will touch our lives and those of our loved ones in a destructive way. God experiences our joy in moments of self-transcendence and beauty. God inspires our compassion, guiding us and the world toward wholeness. God

---

5 I have written about this dynamic relational God in texts such as: *Piglet's Process: Process Theology for All God's Children* (Gonzales, FL: Energion, 2019), *Process Spirituality: Practicing Holy Adventure,* (Gonzales: FL, Energion, 2017), *Process Theology: Embracing Adventure with God* (Gonzales, FL: Energion, 2014, *Process Theology: A Guide for the Perplexed* (London: Continuum, 2011), and Bruce Epperly, *Finding God in Suffering: A Journey with Job* (Gonzales, FL: Energion Publications, 2014).

does not control the future but is reliably present in every moment, giving us guidance and inspiring us to be God's companions in healing the world. The future of our planet, whether it relates to global climate change or the Coronavirus pandemic is open and undecided by God or us. God has not determined what will happen, but is working with us to encourage innovation, compassion, creativity, and solutions not only to this pandemic but to the many other intractable problems we currently face.

I believe God has a vision for this time, and God's vision involves growing solidarity among the peoples of the earth. "In all things God works for good," even things God has not chosen and cannot fully control such as the Coronavirus pandemic (Romans 8:28). I believe that God's vision includes inviting us to go beyond self-interest and nation-first to world loyalty and to sacrificing our rugged individualism to promote the healing of the earth. The outcome of the pandemic and other crises is uncertain, but I am certain that God wants all of us to have abundant life, not just the affluent and privileged, not just North Americans and British, not just human beings. God wants all creation to experience abundance in the context of the greater good of our planet and humankind.

Prophetic Healing. God shapes and guides but does not determine the course of our lives or our health condition. God does not punish us for our imperfections or favor one community over another. Nevertheless, actions have consequences. Part of the panic in North America is related to the impact of nation-first ideologies, blinding our leaders to the intricate interdependence of life and the impact on our nation of what is happening across the globe. Believing we can go it alone as a nation, we find ourselves behind the curve in receiving information and resources from other countries. Moreover, the denial of the Coronavirus by national leaders, much of it politically motivated, lead initially to a failure to implement preventive practices in a timely manner. We do reap what we sow. What we do matters individually and nationally and can shape the course of our personal and planetary health and wellbeing.

The Hebraic prophets and Jesus challenged injustice and inequality. They believed that God felt the joy and pain of humankind and the non-human world and that our unfaithfulness and injustice had serious and individual consequences. Failure to hear God's presence in the cries of the poor deafened the wealthy and powerful to God's voice. The prophet Amos, speaking to a complacent community of political, economic, and religious leaders described the real consequences of injustice in our spiritual lives and the body politic.

> *The time is surely coming, says the Lord God, when I will send a famine on the land; not a famine of bread, or a thirst for water, but of hearing the words of God. They shall wander from sea to sea, and north to east, they shall wander to and fro, seeking the word of God; but they shall not find it.* (Amos 8:11-12)

Despite its spiritual and ethical waywardness, the Hebraic prophets believed that the nation can be redeemed. Today's prophets hold out the same hope for our nation. We must repent our hard-heartedness and nation-first policies. We can turn from self-interest to compassion and care for the least of these. Though not caused by God, the emergence of the Coronavirus is the "handwriting on the wall" for a nation that promotes economic injustice, individualism, and nation-first ideologies. They have been tried and tested and have been found insufficient to protect humanity and the planet. Instead, God's prophetic call to partnership is clear:

> *God has told you, O mortal, what is good, and what does God require of you, but to do justice and to love kindness, and walk humbly with your God.* (Micah 6:8)

> *Take away from me the noise of your songs;*
> *I will not listen to the melody of your harps.*
> *But let justice roll down like waters,*
> *and righteousness like an ever-flowing stream.*
> (Amos 5:23-24)

A Call to Repentance and Action. I write these words on March 15, 2020, a day designated as a National Day of Prayer by the President of the United States. With God's help, we will prevail, proclaimed the President. While it is appropriate for us to look to God for protection and strength, we must remember the words of President Abraham Lincoln, who during another national crisis, asserted that we need to pray to be on God's side rather than seeking to enlist God for our side. God hears the prayers of friend and enemy, and sinner and saint alike.

Prophets of all ages challenge the nation to seek first justice. When the nations of the world are gathered before God, the Creator of the Universe will ask how they treated the "least of these." Our prayer must turn us to care. God is our rock and salvation. But, as we secure the nation from the threat of the Coronavirus, our calling is to go global and to see our own national interest in light of the whole planet. Then God will "crown our good with brotherhood -and sisterhood and personhood — from sea to shining sea."

Practicing Our Faith in a Time Of Pandemic

Though we are tempted to circle the wagons in fear, God wants us to expand the circle of love. God wants us to go beyond binary thinking — in and out, saved and unsaved, and friend and foe. God wants us to see the holiness of all creation, "something of God," as the Quakers say, in everyone.

The Spirit in Me Greets the Spirit in You. Though you may be a self-imposed hermit or have restricted social encounters during the time of pandemic, you can still practice this spiritual exercise. Take a moment to bless everyone you meet, either silently or with words of kindness. Look for the holiness in people walking by your home, newscasters on television, politicians with whom you disagree, and most importantly those with whom you most intimately interact. See the holiness in them, greeting them in silence or with words with God's spirit of peace, affirming their holiness.

With Beauty All Around Us. The Navajo Blessing Way affirms "with beauty all around me I walk." The perception of beauty widens our consciousness, places our fears in a larger life-supporting perspective, and invites us to be beauty-creators with God. Throughout the day, notice beauty. I gaze at the stars as I waken each morning, giving thanks for this one unrepeatable day. "This is the day that God has made and I will rejoice and be glad in it" (Psalm 118:24). After my time of writing and morning prayers, I walk a few miles on a local beach, bathing my senses in beauty. I look out my windows at the evergreens and listen for birdsongs and pause to notice wild turkeys crossing the road in front of my home.

The philosopher Alfred North Whitehead says that the aim of the universe is toward the production of beauty. Beauty is everywhere. Today, commit to being both a beauty finder and love finder, sharing the journey with the Artist of the Universe. Remember this is a season for kindness. With Mother Teresa, you can do something beautiful for God.

With beauty all around me I live. With love all around me I act. Let me see beauty everywhere and bring it forth from difficult places. Let me be a love finder and a beauty giver in all that I do. Amen.

CHAPTER FOUR

GOD IS WITH YOU

Where can I go from your spirit?
Or where can I flee from your presence?
If I ascend to heaven, you are there;
    if I make my bed in Sheol, you are there.
If I take the wings of the morning
    and settle at the farthest limits of the sea,
even there your hand shall lead me,
    and your right hand shall hold me fast.
If I say, "Surely the darkness shall cover me,
    and the light around me become night,"
even the darkness is not dark to you;
the night is as bright as the day,
for darkness is as light to you. (Psalm 139:7-12)

In the previous chapter, we reflected on all the wrong theological answers regarding the Coronavirus, including: 1) asserting that is divine punishment for specific sins, usually cherry-picked such as LGBTQ+ equality, religious pluralism, banning of prayer in school, and not socially acceptable sins, denounced in scripture, economic inequality, poverty, inhospitality to strangers; 2) divine omnipotence (all things good and evil come from God's hand); and 3) predestination (God is in control of everything, thus nullifying human agency in shaping the future). I suggested a lively alternative vision of God as the most moved mover, whose power is relational and not coercive, and who needs our partnership in healing the world. While the vision of a relational, non-coercive God seems, at first, abstract, I contend that the vision of God with us profoundly shapes how we respond to the current Coronavirus pandemic.

Psalm 139 is a meditation on divine relationality and nearness of God in all the seasons of life. In the heights and depths, God is with us. In elation and depression God is with us. In darkness and light God is with us. Not a passive God, but a God whose energy shapes our lives and whose Spirit constantly speaks within us in sighs too deep for words.

The story is told of a child who just couldn't get to sleep one night. His father read stories, sung lullabies, but still the boy was wide awake. Finally, in exasperation the father said, God is with you, don't be afraid. To which his son replied, "I want a God with skin on." That's the God we need shares our joys and sorrows, who — like Jesus — weeps over our nation, and who walks beside us in the darkest valley. The God with skin lets go of every impediment to live among us, empathizing and empowering. The God with skin needs our skin, too. Perhaps, with social distancing, we can't hug and hold hands outside our circle of closest relationships. Our skin can be our voice, our tears of understanding, our empathy, and our spiritual companionship as God's heart in a time of pandemic.

We also need a God with "skin in the game." That is, a God for whom our lives and planet in all their uncertainty matters. It matters to God how we respond to this pandemic, issues of justice, and climate change. Our joys and sorrows matter to God and shape the quality of God's experience. Depending on what we do, God's impact of the world is either decreased or increased. Our wisdom and kindness — and the wisdom and compassion of our political leaders — can be a matter of life or death. Although God never gives up on us, what we do is important to the One to Whom All Hearts are Open and All Desires Known.

Practicing Our Faith in a Time Of Pandemic

We need a God with skin and God needs us to be companions in responding to the COVID-19 Pandemic. Trusting God's care, and recognizing we are not alone, we are inspired to be God's agents of creativity and healing in responding to the Coronavirus.

Divine Companionship in the Darkness. Take time to read Psalm 139:7-12 daily as part of your daily meditations. Begin your time with silence, breathing deeply, finding a center in the cyclone, a still point in the storm. Read the passage twice, savoring every phrase. Ask God to make the scripture come alive for you. In the spirit of the practice of Holy Reading or *Lectio Divina*, consider the following pattern :

28

1) After your time of stillness and reading, and opening to God's wisdom, pause to listen for God's voice in your experience.
2) What words or images emerge in the stillness?
3) What do these words or images mean to you now?
4) Hold the word or image in your heart and mind, pondering ways you can embody this wisdom in this unique time of pandemic and beyond.
5) Conclude with a prayer of thanksgiving.

Thanksgiving for Living. Meister Eckhardt stated that if the only prayer you can make is thank you, that will be enough. Consider the hymn, "Now Thank We All Our God," written by Lutheran pastor Martin Rinkart (circa 1636) in a time of war and plague. As the pastor in Eilenburg, Saxony, a walled city flooded by refugees from the Thirty Years War, Rinkart buried as many as fifty people each day, and four thousand during the year, including his wife. Still, he trusted God to get him through the anguish he felt. Thanksgiving enabled him to experience God's love and providence that embraces us in life, death, and eternity.

Now thank we all our God,
with heart and hands and voices,
Who wondrous things has done,
in Whom this world rejoices;
Who from our mothers' arms
has blessed us on our way
With countless gifts of love,
and still is ours today.

O may this bounteous God
through all our life be near us,
With ever joyful hearts
and blessed peace to cheer us;
And keep us in His grace,
and guide us when perplexed;
And free us from all ills,
in this world and the next!

All praise and thanks to God
the Father now be given;
The Son and Him Who reigns
with Them in highest Heaven;
The one eternal God,
whom earth and Heaven adore;
For thus it was, is now,
and shall be evermore.

Take time to read, sing or listen to this hymn on your phone or computer. Then, take a few minutes in the spirit of the hymn to give thanks for God's presence in your life. What blessings are you experiencing today? Where have you experienced love or beauty today? Where has God called you to deeper faith and compassion? In response to God's goodness, what can you do at this time to bring healing and beauty to the world? Thank God for God's goodness in this time of pandemic.

Thank you, thank you, thank you! For love, life, beauty, wonder, and the chance to reach out to others. Let my gratitude empower me to give hope and love to others, trusting that in life and death, I am yours and that my times are in your hands. Amen.

CHAPTER FIVE

WE ARE CONNECTED

Abide in me as I abide in you. Just as the branch cannot bear fruit by itself unless it abides in the vine, neither can you unless you abide in me. I am the vine, you are the branches. Those who abide in me and I in them bear much fruit, because apart from me you can do nothing. (John 15:4-5)

The Coronavirus has made clear that a world dominated by independent and isolated nation-states is hazardous to our health. No one is an island. Neither is any nation an island. Seas and walls cannot protect us from viruses, pollution, and climate change. When Martin Luther King spoke of the intricate fabric of relatedness, he was primarily speaking of the human community. But his recognition that our wellbeing requires the wholeness of others pertains to the non-human world as well. We live in a world of *ubuntu* — "I am because of you — which embraces every aspect of our lives.

The interdependence of life can be the source of disease or healing for us and our world. The Coronavirus is a disease, fostered by the intricate relatedness of life. What happens in China and Korea shapes what goes on in Cape Cod, London, and Nova Scotia. We live in the world in which a butterfly flapping its wings — or a carpenter diagnosed with Coronavirus in Wuhan — can create panic in Centerville, Massachusetts where I live.

The reality of interdependence can also provide the pathway to healing. Environmentalist Bill McKibben asserts the most important thing an individual can do to respond to climate change is to quit being an individual. This applies to individual nations as well as individual persons. The world is saved, as Jewish mysticism asserts, one person at a time. It is also saved one governmental decision at a time. In a time of pandemic, expanding our circles of compassion and responsibility has now become a necessity. The entire world is in this together, and we must work together, sacred and secular, to heal the earth not just in terms of the Coronavirus but also global climate change.

The Ultimate Relationship. The story is told of the night of the shooting stars. As they saw the falling stars, the villagers ran for their lives. "The sky is falling. We are doomed," they cried. As they ran aimlessly through the village, they came upon the wise women and men of the village. "The stars are falling," they shouted. The wise ones paused and looked at the heavens, and responded, "Yes the stars are falling. But look see all the stars that are standing still."

Tonight, as I drove my grandchildren home, I invited them to look at the sky. I shared my faith that we lived in a grand universe in which God's wisdom endures — like the stars — forever. The author of Lamentations lived through a time of uncertainty. Like the author of Psalm 46, the world as he knew it was at risk. His faith was in God whose love joins the eternal and the temporary, the infinite and the intimate.

> *The steadfast love of the LORD never ceases,*
> *his mercies never come to an end;*
> *they are new every morning;*
> *great is your faithfulness.*
> *"The Lord is my portion," says my soul,*
> *"therefore I will hope in him."* (Lamentations 3:22-23)

Our hope is in the ever-present, ever-loving, ever-active God, moving in and through our lives, providing for deepest needs and sharing our journey sickness and health and death and life. Our ultimate relationship with the faithful God whose "mercies are new every morning." With God as our companion, we can claim with Luther that "in the midst of life, we are surrounded by death, and in the midst of death, we are surrounded by life."

Practicing Our Faith in a Time of Pandemic

Jesus affirmed, "I am the vine and you are the branches." We are all connected in the body of Christ. Our joys and sorrows are one. Our health and wellbeing are related to the wellbeing of our families, companion animals, community, and the planet. Connected to the vine, we have abundant energy, love, and creativity.

Affirmative Faith. The apostle Paul says, "think about these things." Affirmations can change our minds, hearts, and actions. Let us live with spiritual affirmations to enlarge our spirits and give us courage in this time of pandemic.

> *I am connected with the Divine Vine.*
> *God's energy of love flows in and through me.*
> *I bear healthy and loving fruit.*
> *Nothing can separate me from the love of God.*
> *Wherever I am God is present.*
> *I am the light of the world.*
> *My light shines giving healing and joy to all around.*

Practice these affirmations daily. Take a few deep breaths and repeat one or a number of these three times, breathing deeply between each one. Whenever you begin to feel anxious, return to one of these affirmations.

Connected to the Divine Vine. In this spiritual practice, begin with a time of silence, breathing deeply God's Spirit of Connection. Feel yourself connected with God and your loved ones with every breath. Let God's healing and loving energy flow into every cell of your body from head to toe. Feel God's loving energy surrounding you and protecting you. With each exhalation, feel your connection with your friends and loved ones. Let your loving energy connect and nurture them, adding beauty to their lives.

Now, change your focus to the global. Experience God's loving energy come to and through you from the Living Earth. With each breath, feel yourself connected with our Mother Planet. As you exhale, let your healing energy flow from you to your loved ones, church, community, nation, and family.

Kything. Popularized by author Madeleine L'Engle, kything comes from the Scottish word "Kythe," to make visible or to manifest. Kything is grounded in the intricate and gentle interdependence of life, the oneness that connects us, regardless of distance. In my practice of kything, often occurring during my morning beach walks, I follow these steps:

1) *Breathing deeply, feeling my oneness with creation, past, present, and the emerging future. Experiencing my unity with all creation.*
2) *Visualizing myself as embraced by God's love, filling my cells and my soul.*
3) *Visualizing another person or companion animal beside me, sitting, standing, or in my case, walking, feeling their nearness in the spirit, transcending space and time.*
4) *Visualizing each of us joined with every breath, God breathing through me to them and then back to me.*
5) *Closing with a blessing for the one with whom I kythe.*[6]

Loving God, you are the Vine and your energy of love flows in and through me to all creation. Let me experience my connectedness with you and lovingly share my loving energy with others. Amen.

---

6   For more on kything, see Louis Savary, *Kything: The Art of Spiritual Presence* (Mahweh, NJ: Paulist Press, 1989).

CHAPTER SIX

A TIME FOR KINDNESS

Love is patient; love is kind; love is not envious or boastful or arrogant or rude. It does not insist on its own way; it is not irritable or resentful; it does not rejoice in wrongdoing but rejoices in the truth. It bears all things, believes all things, hopes all things, endures all things. Love never ends. (1 Corinthians 13:4-8)

Now is the time for kindness. Kindness among friends and kindness as a national and international policy. Kindness involves the movement from self-interest to care for our family and neighbors to the wider affirmation of community relationships and national wellbeing to widest commitment to world loyalty. The word "kindness" is connected with the word "kinship." The pandemic tells us that we are kin and that our wellbeing depends on kinship with all creation.

The Gospel of Luke relates a story of a conversation between Jesus and a member of the Jewish upper class. (Luke 10:25-37)

Just then a lawyer stood up to test Jesus. "Teacher," he said, "what must I do to inherit eternal life?" He said to him, "What is written in the law? What do you read there?" He answered, "You shall love the Lord your God with all your heart, and with all your soul, and with all your strength, and with all your mind; and your neighbor as yourself." And he said to him, "You have given the right answer; do this, and you will live." But wanting to justify himself, he asked Jesus, "And who is my neighbor?"

Who is my neighbor? Isn't that the key question for persons and communities facing the Coronavirus pandemic? Many of us are going to be sequestered in our homes. Some of us, like myself, have rich relationships with families in our neighborhoods as well as ongoing employment in writing and pastoral ministry. Our lives are, for the moment, safe, privileged, and comfortable. Many others will be alone — single persons, most especially senior adults. Others will be dealing with the challenges of single parenting, trying to hold onto their jobs and take care of their children with little or

35

no support from families and ex-husbands or ex-wives. Still others will be facing the challenges of raising special needs children with virtually no community resources as support systems shutdown due to the risk of contagion. How do we sequester ourselves physically without sequestering ourselves spiritually, emotionally, and relationally? How will we see others as kin, when we are in domestic lockdown? How do we come to see our planet as one large, wonderful, and diverse neighborhood?

Jesus didn't describe the logistics of kindness. He revealed the meaning of kinship in his table fellowship, healing ministry, and welcome to outcasts, ostracized, and marginalized. In response to the lawyer's query, "And who is my neighbor?" Jesus told a story about an outsider who embodied the heart of God's realm of Shalom.

> *A man was going down from Jerusalem to Jericho, and fell into the hands of robbers, who stripped him, beat him, and went away, leaving him half dead. Now by chance a priest was going down that road; and when he saw him, he passed by on the other side. So likewise a Levite, when he came to the place and saw him, passed by on the other side. But a Samaritan while traveling came near him; and when he saw him, he was moved with pity. He went to him and bandaged his wounds, having poured oil and wine on them. Then he put him on his own animal, brought him to an inn, and took care of him. The next day he took out two denarii, gave them to the innkeeper, and said, "Take care of him; and when I come back, I will repay you whatever more you spend."*
>
> *[Then Jesus asked], "Which of these three, do you think, was a neighbor to the man who fell into the hands of the robbers?" The lawyer said, "The one who showed him mercy." Jesus said to him, "Go and do likewise."* (Luke 10:30-37)

The answer is clear to Jesus. "Go and do likewise…show mercy" by breaking down the barriers of individuality, race, clan, citizenship, sexuality, age, and politics. There is no "other," Jesus proclaims. As we face the Coronavirus, we must recognize that we can no longer denigrate the immigrant or undocumented resident. The virus does not discriminate between citizen and non-citizen. The USA's three-year attack on immigrants — both legal and undocumented — has put all US citizens at risk. Fearful of deportation, immigrants may choose not to seek medical care, thus putting the larger community at risk. They may go into hiding, choosing not to work in our farms and processing plants, thus putting our food supply at risk.

The Coronavirus challenges us to go beyond the binary in politics, ethnicity, sexuality, and citizenship. The quest for kindness is political as well as personal and, during this time of pandemic, we must reframe our immigration policy, giving medical amnesty to every undocumented resident and, then, when the pandemic subsides have a clear and immediate path to citizenship for the "dreamers" as well as their parents.

The times call for kindness. We are one in the spirit, we are one in God, and God calls us to ever-expanding circles of compassion and kinship, remembering that as "as you did it to one of the least of these who are members of my family, you did it to me" (Matthew 25:40).

Practicing Our Faith in a Time of Pandemic

Let love be your aim. Crises can either expand our contract our spirits. We can either turn away from life or embrace God's abundant life. This is not a matter of social distancing. There is no distance in prayer! We can love the world from a monastery, a hospital bed, or as a first responder or social activist. In an interdependent world, our feelings of love traverse the universe. Spiritually speaking, we can walk beside persons thousands of miles from us.

Prayerful Interdependence. Sidelined by illness in her mid-seventies social activist Dorothy Day committed herself to a life of prayer — for justice, for peace, and for friends and enemies alike. This week, your travel may be restricted but nothing can restrict prayer. Our prayers radiate across the universe without impediments of space or time.

Throughout the day, stop to pray! Pray for the persons on social media, especially those with whom you disagree. Pray and then post! Pray for national leaders, even those whose perspectives radically differ from your own. Pray for everyone who walks by your home or for everyone with whom you interact. Pray for loved ones, far and near. Pray for the earth.

In the spirit of Psalm 150:6, "let everything that breathes, praise God," breathe your prayers. Let every breath join you with God in healing the world.

A Time for Kindness. A bumper sticker says, "practice random acts of kindness and senseless acts of mercy." Let this be your goal. Begin your day with prayer. Before consulting your local or cable news, immerse yourself in silence, finding a center in the cyclone and peace in the storm. Breathe deeply the peace of God, connecting you with the Beauty and Love that gives birth to creation and every moment of experience. Out of this still and peaceful place, greet everyone with kindness.

Pause to breathe in the Spirit of Love when you are tempted to become impatient or snap at a loved one. Many of us are in closer quarters than usual with our families and though we may need to be intentional about creating space for ourselves — going on a walk, putting on our headphones to listen to music, or finding a quiet spot in our homes — our interactions will be more immediate and intense. Remember that we are all on edge, even when we feel at peace. So, do your best, without guilt, to treat everyone as Christ, as well as to be graceful to your own imperfections.

Let love be your goal in everything you do. Let all creatures, human and non-human be safe and experience God's love. This is a time for kindness, for fear that has said its prayers, and for trust in a Love That Will Not Let Us Go.

Heart of the Universe, let me love more deeply than I can imagine. Let your love flow in me and through me. Let this day and every day be a time for kindness. Let me be your companion in healing the world one moment at a time. Amen.

TOPICAL LINE DRIVES
Straight to the Point in under 44 Pages

All Topical Line Drives volumes are priced at $5.99 print and $2.99 in all ebook formats.

Available

The Authorship of Hebrews: The Case for Paul	David Alan Black
What Protestants Need to Know about Roman Catholics	Robert LaRochelle
What Roman Catholics Need to Know about Protestants	Robert LaRochelle
Forgiveness: Finding Freedom from Your Past	Harvey Brown, Jr.
Process Theology: Embracing Adventure with God	Bruce Epperly
Holistic Spirituality: Life Transforming Wisdom from the Letter of James	Bruce Epperly
To Date or Not to Date: What the Bible Says about Pre-Marital Relationships	D. Kevin Brown
The Eucharist: Encounters with Jesus at the Table	Robert D. Cornwall
The Authority of Scripture in a Postmodern Age: Some Help from Karl Barth	Robert D. Cornwall
Rendering unto Caesar	Chris Surber
The Caregiver's Beattitudes	Robert Martin
What is Wrong with Social Justice	Elgin Hushbeck, Jr.
I'm Right and You're Wrong	Steve Kindle
Words of Woe: Alternative Lectionary Texts	Robert D. Cornwall
Stewardship: God's Way of Recreating the World	Steve Kindle
Those Footnotes in Your New Testament	Thomas W. Hudgins
Jonah: When God Changes	Bruce G. Epperly
Ruth & Esther: Women of Agency and Adventure	Bruce G. Epperly

... and many others!

Generous Quantity Discounts Available
Dealer Inquiries Welcome
Energion Publications — P.O. Box 841
Gonzalez, FL 32560
Website: http://energionpubs.com
Phone: (850) 525-3916

ALSO FROM ENERGION PUBLICATIONS

Finding God in Suffering
A Journey with Job

Finding God in Suffering is a wise, honest, and liberating approach to one of the most difficult questions we face.

Patricia Adams Farmer
Author of
Embracing a Beautiful God

Bruce G. Epperly

BY BRUCE EPPERLY

Taking theology seriously again — with a stuffed animal!

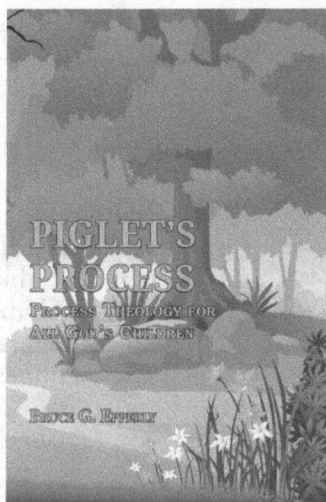

PIGLET'S PROCESS
PROCESS THEOLOGY FOR ALL GOD'S CHILDREN

BRUCE G. EPPERLY

MORE FROM ENERGION PUBLICATIONS

Personal Study

Holy Smoke! Unholy Fire	Bob McKibben	$14.99
The Jesus Paradigm	David Alan Black	$17.99
When People Speak for God	Henry Neufeld	$17.99
The Sacred Journey	Chris Surber	$11.99

Christian Living

Faith in the Public Square	Robert D. Cornwall	$16.99
Grief: Finding the Candle of Light	Jody Neufeld	$8.99
Crossing the Street	Robert LaRochelle	$16.99
Life in the Spirit	J. Hamilton Weston	$12.99

Bible Study

Learning and Living Scripture	Lentz/Neufeld	$12.99
Inspiration: Hard Questions, Honest Answers	Alden Thompson	$29.99
Colossians & Philemon	Allan R. Bevere	$12.99
Ephesians: A Participatory Study Guide	Robert D. Cornwall	$9.99

Theology

Christian Archy	David Alan Black	$9.99
The Politics of Witness	Allan R. Bevere	$9.99
Ultimate Allegiance	Robert D. Cornwall	$9.99
From Here to Eternity	Bruce Epperly	$5.99
The Journey to the Undiscovered Country	William Powell Tuck	$9.99
Eschatology: A Participatory Study Guide	Edward W. H. Vick	$9.99
The Adventist's Dilemma	Edward W. H. Vick	$14.99

Ministry

Clergy Table Talk	Kent Ira Groff	$9.99
Thrive	Ruth Fletcher	$14.99
Out of the Office: A Theology of Ministry	Bob Cornwall	$9.99

Generous Quantity Discounts Available
Dealer Inquiries Welcome
Energion Publications — P.O. Box 841
Gonzalez, FL_ 32560
Website: http://energionpubs.com
Phone: (850) 525-3916

www.ingramcontent.com/pod-product-compliance
Lightning Source LLC
Chambersburg PA
CBHW011748020426
42331CB00014B/3318